Collaborative Practices for Educators
Six Keys to Effective Communication

Patty Lee, Ed.[

CORWIN PRESS
A SAGE Publications Company
Thousand Oaks, CA 91320

KH

For information:

Corwin Press
A SAGE Company
2455 Teller Road
Thousand Oaks, California 91320
www.corwinpress.com

SAGE Ltd.
1 Oliver's Yard
55 City Road
London EC1Y 1SP
United Kingdom

SAGE India Pvt. Ltd.
B 1/I 1 Mohan Cooperative
   Industrial Area
Mathura Road, New Delhi 110 044
India

SAGE Asia-Pacific Pte. Ltd.
33 Pekin Street #02-01
Far East Square
Singapore 048763

Printed in the United States of America.

ISBN: 978-1-890455-05-9
       1-890455-05-9

This book is printed on acid-free paper.

07   08   09   10   11   10 9 8 7 6 5 4 3 2 1

7/29/08

TABLE OF CONTENTS

FOREWORD

WE are the resources for collaboration in today's schools. **WE** are the agents of change. No matter what innovation is challenging us, no matter what mandate is required, **PEOPLE** are at the center and **COMMUNICATION** is the foundation. When we know how to communicate effectively with one another, we open more doors to meet the needs of the students in our charge. When we work together in collaborative teams, we create a better future for ourselves and our students.

The Need for Collaboration

Today's schools are expected to be more inclusive than ever before. The students who arrive at our doorsteps are increasingly diverse with a wide range of needs. Students come with identified special needs, different learning styles, English as a second language, and all levels of preparation, support, and readiness. Faculty are asked to work in teams to address these different and sometimes conflicting needs. No longer can a teacher close the door and just teach. Teachers must serve on grade level teams, interdisciplinary teams, parent-teacher teams, content area teams, and student support teams. When these teams work well together, ideas abound and effective interventions are created. However, when these teams are dysfunctional, energy is wasted and misunderstandings can lead to less than satisfactory working relationships. We as educators must learn to work collaboratively, placing the students at the center of our efforts. In essence we must learn to respectfully "mind each other's business".

This book is written to assist teachers in their collaboration with colleagues, parents, students, and administrators. The strategies and practices presented are drawn from over 40 years experience in the fields of general and special education. Teachers, paraprofessionals, specialists, parents, and students have contributed to these ideas by sharing their stories, suggestions, successes, and mistakes. As you try the strategies and practices in this book, you will become aware of which communication skills you are naturally good at and which ones you may want to improve. You will learn how to apply what you already KNOW to what you DO.

About this Book

This book is based upon the premise that we are often more collaborative with our students than we are with our adult colleagues. We use effective communication skills more naturally with our students than we may with the parents, paraprofessionals, and other teachers with whom we work. We listen more closely to students, we ask more meaningful questions, we attempt to understand where our students are "coming from", we put energy into explaining ourselves and we watch for indications of misunderstanding. On the other hand, we often are much more casual in our communication with adults. We may find ourselves interrupting more often, putting energy into getting our own point across rather than attempting to understand theirs, listening halfheartedly and not giving much thought to how we express ourselves. These are habits that occur frequently among adults who work together and they interfere with effective communication. When we learn to use effective communication skills with adult colleagues, as we do with our students, we build the foundation for collaboration.

The first chapter addresses the challenges in communication and collaboration that typically occur when adults are assigned to work together in teams. The following chapters of the book are devoted to the six keys of effective communication:

1. Developing Expectations--Anticipating and predicting outcomes.

2. Preparing Ahead--Planning ahead and gathering resources to enhance the interaction.

3. Understanding Perspectives--Acknowledging, recognizing, and respecting a diversity of opinions.

4. Asking Questions--Inquiring and seeking more information.

5. Listening--Making a conscious effort to hear and understand what is said.

6. Speaking Clearly--Sending a message that is received as it was meant.

Each chapter begins by describing what we know about the title aspect of communication and why it is important. It continues with a chart delineating the differences of how we use this skill with kids compared to what typically happens in our interactions with adults. As the chapter continues, the author presents 10 strategies that will guide you in developing this particular aspect of your communication skills. Within each of the ten strategies are three suggested practices for use in your educational setting. The practices are divided into those you can do on your own, with another person, and within a group. This book includes 60 strategies and 180 practices to assist with developing your skills in communication and collaboration.

Using this Book

The book is structured so that you can work on any of the six areas of communication and in any order you prefer. You can try some of the ideas by yourself if you are not ready to try them with another person. You can suggest to your grade level or content area team that you practice some of the ideas together. You can focus on just one area of communication or several at once.

Throughout the book you will find sections to record your reflections related to the areas and skills you want to practice. When you decide to use one of the practices, it is helpful to record what you did, how you felt, and what you learned in the interaction. It is also important to note what worked and did not work for you. Do not expect to change all of your communication behaviors overnight. As with the implementation of any meaningful change, it will take time and practice before it becomes internal. Be patient with yourself and note the gradual shift to more satisfying and effective communication.

The book is an exceptional resource to be used for staff development or to incorporate into in-service training for educational teams. Educators can use this as a tool to discuss their current communication practices. Often by incorporating only a few of the changes, educational teams will note a significant improvement in group communication. The suggested practices can also be used as discussion starters and additional strategies may be designed which are specific to the particular school setting and current issues within the setting. Secondary and post secondary educators will find this book full of activities that can be adapted to teach effective communication skills to their students. The strategies and practices in this book are meant to be generic so that they lend themselves to application in all educational settings.

It is my hope that teachers will find this book useful as they work collaboratively with their colleagues in the service of our children and youth.

Patty Lee, Ed.D.
Author

The Challenges of Collaboration

Oh, the Assumptions We Make!

It is no wonder that many educators face challenges as they work on various teams in our schools. They are expected to work on grade level, content area, and student support teams with little or no training in group process, communication skills, or collaborative problem-solving. These team assignments are often an implicit part of a teacher's job without explicit training to prepare them to function effectively. There is a significant and often false assumption made that all of us know how to work in teams for the good of students.

So, teachers end up on teams and bring their own communication habits along with them, sometimes effective and other times not. Some are comfortable with speaking whereas others are more introverted and rarely voice an opinion. Some members have a need for control; some are task masters, and others prefer for the decision-making to evolve in an organic fashion. Misperceptions can abound. One team member feels that she is doing all of the work; another just wants to teach and doesn't really value all of this "collaboration stuff". This is fertile ground for misunderstandings and divisiveness rather than the hoped for collaborative outcomes.

What We Really Need

For teams to function effectively, members need to:

- reach a common understanding of their goals,
- appreciate the complex process of collaborative problem-solving, and
- become conscious of the individual strengths and weaknesses they bring to teamwork.

When these conditions are met, collaborative teamwork can be a joy and the outcomes far more satisfying than that which any one of the members could have reached alone. In essence, teachers need to be working with their colleagues in the ways that they work with their students.

Meanwhile, Back in the Classroom

Most teachers will tell you that they often work far more collaboratively with their students than with their colleagues. We practice the 6 keys to effective communication in our classrooms almost without thinking about it. We take time in considering the classroom environment and how it might be set up for the most effective communication. We imagine how the students will react to our assignments and we prepare accordingly. We bend down to listen carefully to what they say. We look for any signs of understanding. We think before we speak so that we can send a message effectively. We inquire regularly about how they are, who they are, and what they need. In essence, we are immersed in collaboration.

Bridging the Gap

So how do teachers learn to bring the effective communication skills they are using with students to their interactions with peers? How do teachers learn to listen better, express themselves effectively, and develop collaborative problem-solving skills? As with most change, people need first to realize there is a gap between what they are doing and what needs to be done. Then they can assess which areas they want to develop in becoming more effective in communication.

After this it is a matter of practice; conscious, goal-driven practice. Too many times, our interactions in collegial teams are habitual and personality-driven. If we like everyone on the team, we get along quite well and work cooperatively. However, if we have a conflict with certain members, we revert to our habits of devaluing those members' contributions, competing to get our ideas across, and generally siding with the people with whom we agree.

As we practice new skills, we need to be deliberate and authentic, based upon each person's desire to become an effective team member. Sometimes we will see a difference right away; other times the attempt to change will feel awkward and ineffective. The practice of using the *6 Keys of Effective Communication* can help us break our ineffective habits and build new skills that will add value to the work of the team. As we develop our listening, understanding and speaking skills, we offer new possibilities in collaborative problem-solving. *So let's get started!*

Use this page to write down ideas that might come to mind while reading/referring to this guide.
Remember, collaboration begins with each one of us making ourselves accessible to others.

First Key

DEVELOPING EXPECTATIONS

You'll see it when you believe it

Wayne Dyer, 1989, Avon Books

DEVELOPING EXPECTATIONS

What We Know

To develop expectations is to anticipate, think ahead, and predict occurrences and outcomes.

★ Developing expectations gives us a sense of control and confidence in relationship to future events.

★ When we develop expectations, we become pro-active rather than reactive in our interactions.

★ Thinking ahead about communication with others can assist us in producing positive outcomes rather than leaving it to chance.

★ Predicting a variety of possible occurrences challenges us to generate a range of responses which can lead to increased flexibility.

★ Anticipating the dynamics of an interaction can increase our ability to be more accepting of differing points of view.

Developing Expectations – What We DO

WHAT WE OFTEN DO with KIDS	WHAT WE SOMETIMES DO with ADULTS
Set high expectations for our students	Set few expectations for our work with our peers
Explain/Co-create classroom rules and standards of behavior	Conduct our meetings in ways they've always been conducted with no agreed upon code of conduct
Discuss and display ground rules for participation	Expect newcomers to "figure out" the ground rules
Consider time allotments for task completion; make assignments accordingly	Attempt to "fit" the task into a prescribed time slot (one-hour meeting after school)
Determine what times of day will be best for what types of learning	Assume that the traditional time allotted is all we have
Assess the interpersonal dynamics for effective instructional grouping	Recognize, accept, and figure that "what you see is what you get"
Formulate student-teacher roles and responsibilities according to the context	Allow and let the traditional role (e.g. psychologist) determine the responsibilities (psychometric assessment)
Anticipate daily crises, interruptions, and delays	Expect the meeting to follow the set agenda in a predetermined amount of time
Predict that we will need to accommodate for individual learning differences	Expect everyone to process information the way we do

Strategies for Developing Expectations

1. Develop an agreed upon set of ground rules for effective communication in professional meetings.

2. Orient new members and guests to ground rules.

3. Anticipate what people with different points of view might say and how you might respond.

4. State aloud what you believe you can or cannot accomplish in an allotted amount of time.

5. Generate member expectations at the beginning of a meeting.

6. Establish regular times for reviewing roles and responsibilities, (e.g., once a semester).

7. Ask colleagues what they expect from students, from parents, and from you.

8. Keep a reflective log of communication interactions and analyze the log for progress, patterns, and themes.

9. Visualize your next communication interaction as positive and productive.

10. Anticipate potential communication breakdowns that could occur in your teamwork.

Strategies and Practices for Developing Expectations

| Strategy 1 | **Develop an agreed upon set of ground rules for effective communication at professional meetings.** |

Individual

Note your own speaking and listening skills at meetings. What could you do differently at the next meeting that would improve your communication? Do it.

Reflection _____

_____

Colleague

Have a discussion with a colleague who attends the same meetings as you. Ask "What would improve our communication at these meetings?" Take the suggestions to the larger group.

Reflection _____

_____

Group

Have each person complete the following sentence: "Our team communication would improve significantly if we ...". Post all responses on a flip chart and discuss which ones are "doable." Have each person rank their top 3 and total the rankings to obtain the top 3 for the entire group. Commit to doing these.

Reflection _____

_____

| Strategy 2 | **Orient new members and guests to ground rules.** |

Individual

Take it upon yourself to talk with parents about parent conferences before they start. Let them know how much time is allotted for the conference and what they can expect from you.

Reflection _____

_____

Colleague

Most IEP meetings include a guest (someone who does not attend such meetings on a regular basis such as parents, students, general education teachers, or a community representative). Select one person from the core team to handle introductions and to inform guests of the ground rules and typical process.

Reflection _____

_____

Group

Assign someone on your grade level team to orient new members to typical meeting protocol.

Reflection _____

_____

| Strategy 3 | *Anticipate what people with different points of view might say and how you might respond.* |

Individual

Identify a colleague with whom you often disagree. Write 5 questions you could ask this person to get him or her to elaborate on an opinion.

*Reflection*_____

_____

Colleague

Talk with two people with differing perspectives on an issue. During the interaction make sure that you ask questions and refrain from making comments. Consider how you would mediate a discussion between these two people.

Reflection _____

_____

Group

Bring clarity to the different points of view on an issue your team is dealing with. Make a rule of no commente, just listening to one another. Have each person state how they feel, what they think and believe about this issue.

Reflection _____

_____

Strategy 4   *State aloud what you believe you can or cannot accomplish in an allotted amount of time.*

Individual

When a colleague asks to speak to you and you are unable to give your full attention (e.g., in a hurry, preoccupied, or distracted), respond by saying, "I want to listen to what you are saying, but I'm unable to give you my full attention right now. Could we talk at a later time?"

Reflection _____

_____

Colleague

When you begin a planning session with a colleague (e.g., developing a thematic unit for team-teaching) say something such as, "I brought some materials. I would like for us to see if we want to use them. What do you want for us to accomplish in this session?"

Reflection _____

_____

Group

At the beginning of an IEP meeting, begin the meeting with, "Today, we hope to review (student's) progress and make decisions about future services. We have about one hour to do this. If we don't accomplish what we need to do in the allotted time, we'll schedule another session."

Reflection _____

_____

Strategy 5 *Generate member expectations at the beginning of a meeting.*

Individual

Write down what you expect will happen in the next interaction with a colleague you find challenging; what he will say/do-what you will say/do. After the interaction, note in writing how accurate your predictions were.

Reflection _____

_____

Colleague

Prior to a parent-teacher conference, send a form asking the parent(s) to write three questions they have about their child's progress to bring the completed form to the conference. Ask the parents to read their questions at the beginning of the meeting. Write the questions on paper or a flip chart so they can be referred to through-out the conference.

Reflection _____

_____

Group

Have each person attending the team meeting write one thing they hope to accomplish at the meeting. During the first five minutes read these aloud to see if you're on common ground.

Reflection _____

_____

Strategy 6	*Establish regular times for reviewing roles and responsibilities (e.g., once a semester).*

Individual

At the beginning of the school year, write each of the roles you believe your job entails (teacher, consultant, parent, peer support, friend). Beside each of the roles, write the responsibilities that are inherent in that role.

Roles	Responsibilities

Reflection _____

_____

Colleague

When team teaching classes, create a yearly calendar that delineates periodic checkpoints to review responsibilities such as grading, contacting parents, disciplining, and communicating with other staff.

Reflection _____

_____

Group

On a quarterly basis, have the IEP team review individual roles in relation to the IEP meetings. Discuss joint responsibilities for communicating with parents, reporting progress at IEP meetings, using jargon free language, and preparing students to participate in IEP meetings.

Reflection _____

_____

Strategy 7 — *Ask colleagues what they expect from students, from parents, and from you.*

Individual

Formulate several ways to ask colleagues what their expectations are, such as, "Tell me about how you organize your classroom," and "What kind of contact would you like to have with parents?"

Reflection _____

_____

Colleague

Ask the questions from the above Individual Practice Activity and listen carefully to the answer. Ask additional questions to prompt your colleague to elaborate further, such as, "What have you found that doesn't work in your classroom?" and "What has worked for you in parent involvement?"

Reflection _____

_____

Group

At a faculty meeting discuss "How we would like our students to describe us." Then talk about what behaviors on the part of the staff would lead to such perceptions.

Reflection _____

_____

Strategy 8 ***Keep a reflective log of communication interactions. Analyze the log for progress, patterns and themes.***

Individual

Keep a daily journal for one month, noting the colleagues with whom you interact. Are there some colleagues with whom you rarely communicate?

Reflection _____

_____

Colleague

Think of someone with whom you collaborate on a regular basis. Is the communication equal or is one person more dominant? Would you like for that to change?

Reflection _____

_____

Group

During a meeting, calculate the number of statements made compared to the number of questions asked.

Reflection _____

_____

Strategy 9 ***Visualize your next communication interaction as positive and productive.***

Individual

Set a timer for five minutes. Write as quickly as you can all the ways you can think of to communicate clearly. Don't concern yourself with spelling, punctuation, or duplication. After five minutes, read through the list and visualize the settings where you most often use these communication abilities.

Reflection _____

_____

Colleague

Imagine you are in conversation with a colleague with whom you often disagree. Picture yourself as a good listener, taking into consideration your colleagues' point of view, and then clearly stating how you see the issue differently.

Reflection _____

_____

Group

Visualize yourself in your classroom presenting a lesson, clearly and with confidence. Now imagine the audience as a group of your peers and that your presentation continues to be clear and confident.

Reflection _____

_____

Strategy 10 *Anticipate potential communication breakdowns that could occur in your teamwork.*

Individual

Think about a behavior of a colleague which you find irritating and "pushes your buttons". Examine what you typically do in response to this behavior. What might you do differently next time?

Reflection _____

_____

Colleague

Ask a colleague to read a note you are planning to send home to parents. Have them give you their opinion of the tone and clarity of the note.

Reflection _____

_____

Group

Think about a recent meeting where communication broke down and you did not say anything. What do you wish you would have said? Imagine saying it next time.

Reflection _____

_____

Use this page to write down ideas that might come to mind while reading/referring to this guide.
Remember, collaboration begins with each one of us making ourselves accessible to others.

Second Key

PREPARING AHEAD

If you always do what you've always done, you'll always get what you've always gotten. Is it enough?

Author Unknown

PREPARING AHEAD

What We Know

To prepare ahead is to plan in advance what physical, mental, human, and material resources might be needed to increase the effectiveness of the upcoming lesson, meeting, or interaction.

★ Preparing materials in advance reduces the likelihood we will have to take away from meeting time to get these materials.

★ Changing the physical arrangements can help prompt new ways of thinking. Arranging furniture ahead of time and in a variety of ways conveys that consideration has been given to the type of meeting.

★ Thinking ahead about the questions we have (not just the points we want to make) assists us in creating a meaningful dialogue with our co-workers.

★ Preparing ahead so that the next meeting will be more effective than the last, increases the likelihood of positive change.

★ Planning ahead often results in a general sense of readiness and direction for team members.

Preparing Ahead – What We DO

WHAT WE OFTEN DO with KIDS	WHAT WE SOMETIMES DO with ADULTS
Decide/think about what to say	Say the first thing that comes to mind
Think about how to introduce an idea	Just start talking without thinking of how we might begin
Prepare according to the learning outcomes we want	Disregard our desired outcomes (outcomes is often just to get it done)
Plan what questions to ask	Prepare what we'll say not what we'll ask
Select what materials will be used	Use the existing forms to guide the meeting
Consider possible room arrangements depending upon the lesson	Meet in the same arrangement time after time
Seek out human and material resources that will supplement (support) the lesson	Assume that routine members will be the only ones needed
Design practice activities to reinforce new skills	Assume we have the skills we need and there's no need for practice
Determine how to evaluate learning progress	Neglect to consider what the team is learning
Expect to monitor and respond to feedback from students so that we can improve the lesson	Persist in conducting business in habitual ways regardless of feedback

Strategies for Preparing Ahead

1. Establish a process where adults review and recommend the best places and room arrangements for meetings.

2. Develop the agenda for meetings based on the participants' questions and concerns.

3. Review on a regular basis team members' material and experiential resources.

4. Develop a process for observing and assessing "meeting" behaviors.

5. Review the purpose or desired outcome of different types of meetings.

6. Set annual goals for the purpose of improving communication.

7. Devise methods of tracking progress on annual communication goals.

8. Establish practices for obtaining feedback from parents, colleagues, and administrators.

9. Create new ways to think about traditional practices.

10. Use scheduled breaks during the year for predicting communication needs that might arise.

Strategies and Practices for Preparing Ahead

| Strategy 1 | **Establish a process where adults review and recommend the best places and arrangements for meetings.** |

Individual

Picture a recent meeting you were in. How was the room arranged? Could people see each other? What physical barriers interfered with communication? What could you do to improve the arrangement?

Reflection _____

_____

Colleague

Before your next meeting with a co-worker, choose a place that is different from where you typically meet. Think about ways to control possible distractions.

Reflection _____

_____

Group

After one of your standard meetings (e.g. grade level team meeting) ask members if the setting and arrangement are conducive to good communication. Encourage people to make suggestions about other possible places, arrangements, etc.

Reflection _____

_____

Strategy 2   *Develop the agenda for meetings based on the participants' questions and concerns.*

Individual

What information would you like from the parent of one of your students? How could you ask questions that would elicit this information?

Reflection _____

_____

Colleague

Think about three ways to ask a colleague about the next curriculum unit you will be working on. Write down the questions. Plan to ask at least one of the questions the next time you meet.

Reflection _____

_____

Group

Ask faculty members to write a question for the entire faculty to discuss. Place the questions in a central location. Discuss 2 or 3 questions at each faculty meeting throughout the year.

Reflection _____

_____

Strategy 3 ***Review on a regular basis team members' material and experiential resources.***

Individual

Keep a listing of outside community resource people who might be available to help with creative programming for your school.

Reflection _____

_____

Colleague

After attending a workshop or conference, share the information with a colleague, highlighting the sessions that you attended. Offer to make copies of the information received. Find ways to share with entire faculty.

Reflection _____

_____

Group

Set aside one of your regularly scheduled team meetings to brainstorm the areas of competencies within the team (e.g. behavior management, cooperative learning, team-teaching). Post the list in a central location and update it at least twice a year.

Reflection _____

_____

Strategy 4	*Develop a process for observing and assessing communication which occurs during meetings.*

Individual

During an IEP meeting, keep track of the acronyms (IEP, OT, PT, LD, etc.) that are used. Was there anyone at the meeting who might not know what those acronyms mean?

Reflection _____

_____

Colleague

At a departmental meeting, ask members what would improve the communication at these meetings. List the ones you want to work on first.

Reflection _____

_____

Group

Designate a faculty person to observe and record the communication interactions at a faculty meeting. Which are enhancing communication and which are impeding it? What needs to be changed?

Reflection _____

_____

Strategy 5 — *Review the purpose or desired outcomes of different types of meetings*

Individual

Think about how you would like a parent to describe you after a parent conference. How might you behave so that the parent would describe you this way?

Reflection _____

_____

Colleague

With a colleague, before a planning session, individually write what you hope to accomplish at the session. Read the lists to each other. Prioritize the list together.

Reflection _____

_____

Group

In preparing for a committee or department meeting, plan to ask everyone in the meeting what they believe is the current task at hand. Note similarities and differences among responses.

Reflection _____

_____

Strategy 6   *Set annual goals for the purpose of improving communication.*

Individual

Ask yourself, "What is one thing I could do now to significantly improve my communication skills?" Set a goal related to the behavior.

Reflection _____

_____

Colleague

Discuss with a co-worker the current paperwork you are both doing. Could any of it be omitted, revised, or combined for efficiency and effectiveness? If so, set a timeline for making the changes or recommending the changes to the appropriate personnel.

Reflection _____

_____

Group

Ask your grade level team to respond to a checklist of how communication is going in your meetings (e.g., stating the purpose of the meeting, summarizing main points, checking for understanding). Set goals around the areas that members rank the lowest.

Reflection _____

_____

Strategy 7 *Devise methods of tracking progress in communication.*

Individual

Once you have set a communication goal, write it. Devise a way to track daily the number of opportunities you had for practice and then the number of times you actually practiced the new behavior.

Reflection _____

_____

Colleague

After any new form of paperwork is developed, ask the key people (those who will use the form), for feedback on its readability and clarity.

Reflection _____

_____

Group

Post the goals you set in Group Activity of Strategy 6 in a prominent place where you typically hold grade level team meetings.. Review your progress at least three times a year.

Reflection _____

_____

| Strategy 8 | ***Establish practices for obtaining feedback from parents, colleagues, and administrators.*** |

Individual

Discuss with your students how they view you as a listener. How do they think you could be a better listener?

Reflection _____

_____

Colleague

When you present with a colleague (to the faculty, at a conference) decide together the type of feedback desired and how the information will be obtained.

Reflection _____

_____

Group

Ask parents and regular educators to evaluate the IEP meeting process from their points of view. What would they suggest for improving communication and making the process more "user-friendly".

Reflection _____

_____

Strategy 9   *Create new ways to think about traditional practices*.

Individual

The next time you get an unexpected "free" hour (an appointment is canceled, a meeting is postponed, etc.) fill the free hour with something you love to do instead of something you have to get done.

Reflection _____

_____

Colleague

Think of five people with whom you work on a daily basis. Designate Monday for one, Tuesday for another, etc. On each day of the following week, make sure that you connect with that day's person in a meaningful way.

Reflection _____

_____

Group

Conduct your next committee, planning, departmental, or faculty meeting off school grounds.

Reflection _____

_____

Strategy 10 *Use scheduled breaks during the year for predicting communication needs that might arise*.

Individual

At the end of the first quarter, think about the way you could arrange the chairs and tables differently for parent conferences. Consider an arrangement that would facilitate effective communication.

Reflection _____

_____

Colleague

Meet with a colleague for breakfast or lunch during one of your school breaks. Discuss what you both believe will come up during second semester that will need good, clear communication.

Reflection _____

_____

Group

As a faculty, discuss the challenges in communicating with parents. Brainstorm ideas for creating as collaborative a climate as possible.

Reflection _____

_____

Third Key

UNDERSTANDING PERSPECTIVES

There is nothing so unequal as the equal treatment of unequals.

Author Unknown

UNDERSTANDING PERSPECTIVES

What We Know

To understand perspectives is to acknowledge that everyone sees the world through his own view and to recognize that comprehending those diverse views will serve communication in positive and productive ways.

★ Understanding a persons' perspective conveys respect and opens the lines of communication.

★ Taking diverse perspectives during problem solving increases the possibility of developing mutually satisfying outcomes.

★ Utilizing multiple perspectives can result in creating a variety of new responses and alternatives that would not be available from any single perspective.

★ Considering other perspectives and responding accordingly is simply "treating others as we would like to be treated ourselves".

Understanding Expectations-What We DO

WHAT WE OFTEN DO with KIDS	WHAT WE SOMETIMES DO with ADULTS
Recognize that they'll have a bad day now and then	Act like everyday is about the same
Accept that their emotional state will affect their productivity	Expect about the same productivity across time
Ask how they are when we perceive they're troubled	Avoid interacting or bringing up that they might be troubled.
Cut them some slack when we know of difficult circumstances in their lives	Expect them to leave their difficulties at home
Respond with empathy to a tough situations	Mind our own business
Accept that kids are at varying levels of skill development. What is hard for one may be easy for another	Expect adults to be similarly competent, confident, and productive
Demonstrate patience when they're trying something new	Fail to recognize they might be trying something new
Ask questions to determine "where they're coming from"	Make assumptions about "where they're coming from"
See it as a positive challenge when they disagree with us	Take it personally when they disagree with us

Strategies for Understanding Perspectives

1. Develop ways to encourage others to explain their perspectives.

2. Listen actively to people who have differing perspectives.

3. Learn about differences in adult learning styles.

4. Develop habits that increase understanding and decrease judgment.

5. Develop ways of thinking and speaking that are inclusive rather than exclusive.

6. Become a good observer of people.

7. Increase awareness of "self talk".

8. Read with the purpose of understanding opposing points of view on a controversial issue.

9. Develop new ways to get to know people.

10. Discover the importance of silence.

Strategies and Practices for Understanding Perspectives

Strategy 1	***Develop ways to encourage others to explain their perspectives***

Individual

Think about things people do and say that encourage you to explain your perspective. Write these down. Add to the list as you hear other examples.

Reflection _____

_____

Colleague

The next time someone is expressing a perspective different from your own, urge them to elaborate.

Reflection _____

_____

Group

At a team meeting, bring in someone who is not regularly on the team (e.g. a parent). Ask that person to give you their perspective on whatever issue you've been dealing with (e.g. student portfolios).

Reflection _____

_____

Strategy 2 *Listen actively to people who have differing perspectives.*

Individual

Listen to a talk show host whose beliefs are usually opposite from yours. Write down what you would say in a debate with this person.

Reflection _____

_____

Colleague

When conversing with a colleague who often has a different point of view, ask a question directly linked to what they just said.

Reflection _____

_____

Group

Ask each person in the group to finish a sentence such as, "Our group would function better if we_____." As each person shares their response, compare the similarities and differences.

Reflection _____

_____

Strategy 3 *Learn about adult learning and communication styles.*

Individual

Check bookstores and libraries for information on Adult Learning Styles. Popular authors include Gregorc, Kersey, Kolb, Myers-Briggs. Fill out one of the questionnaires. Read the authors' interpretation. Reflect on how you come across to others.

Reflection _____

_____

Colleague

Identify a co-worker who you think has a different style than yours. Read about the values, preferences, and behaviors of that style. How do you see those characteristics in your co-workers' daily behaviors?

Reflection _____

_____

Group

See if your faculty or team would be interested assessing learning styles together. Arrange for all members to take the inventory, assess the groups' strengths and weaknesses, and discuss the type of implications the results may have in day to day communication.

Reflection _____

_____

Strategy 4 *Develop habits that increase understanding and decrease judgment*

Individual

When you are just about to change a radio or TV station because you don't like what is on, listen or watch for one more minute. With as much neutrality as possible, imagine who would like this and why?

Reflection _____

_____

Colleague

The next time a colleague suggests an idea you don't think will work, ask the person to tell you more. As they elaborate, listen with the intention of fully understanding the idea.

Reflection _____

_____

Group

Ask each person in the group (faculty, team, or committee) to bring a childhood photo and share a "story" from that part of their life.

Reflection _____

_____

Strategy 5 — Develop ways of thinking and speaking that are inclusive rather than exclusive

Individual

Before meeting with a team member about a student you have in common, make a list of all the things you both probably want for the student.

Reflection _____

_____

Colleague

When exchanging ideas with a colleague, try replacing the word "but" with the word "and." For example: instead of saying "That's a good idea, but" say "That's a good idea, and I'm concerned about ..."

Reflection _____

_____

Group

When planning an IEP staffing, ask each person to think of someone, who is not a regular member, whom you could invite to help solve the problem.

Reflection _____

_____

Strategy 6   *Become a good observer of people.*

Individual

Immediately following a stressful interaction at work, write down all the feelings you had during the interaction. Reflect on your behaviors. What did you do? What did you say? Resist judging yourself, just observe.

Reflection _____

_____

Colleague

Think about a person at work with whom you work closely. In your next interaction with him, notice how he communicates. How rapidly does he speak? How does he show he is listening (or not)? What questions does he ask? What type of statements does he make?

Reflection _____

_____

Group

At one of your typical team meetings, pay attention to the group interaction instead of actively participating. (You can say that you just don't feel up to participating). Watch for the following: the person who speaks the most and the one who speaks the least; the person who seems to be influential and the one who does not; the person who listens well and the one who interrupts.

Reflection _____

_____

Strategy 7   *Increase awareness of "self-talk"*

Individual

Pick one day to write down most of the things you say to yourself. For example: "Don't forget to...", "I need to...", "I wish I hadn't said that..." Review the list of statements and note what themes emerge (e.g. To-Do's, Put-Downs). Are they past, present, or future-oriented?

Reflection _____

_____

Colleague

When you talk with others at work, what internal messages are you listening to? Are you attending more to your own "self-talk" than to the person who is speaking?

Reflection _____

_____

Group

During a faculty meeting, what are you saying or asking yourself that you are not saying aloud? Would any of these thoughts, if said aloud, result in improved communication?

Reflection _____

_____

Strategy 8   *Read with the purpose of understanding opposing points of view on a controversial issue*

Individual

Read two opposing letters to the editor. Imagine how each person came to his or her beliefs.

Reflection _____

_____

Colleague

Arrange with a colleague to read two articles with opposing points of view on a controversial subject (e.g. standard-based education, sex education, or inclusive education). Discuss your reactions to the opinions.

Reflection _____

_____

Group

Ask each person in the team, to read an article that presents differing points of view on a central theme (e.g. standards-based education, inclusive education, or assessment). Follow up with a team discussion regarding ideas and opinions.

Reflection _____

_____

Strategy 9   *Develop new ways to get to know your co-workers*

Individual

Think about something that you love to do outside of work which few of your colleagues know. Mention this to a few people in casual conversation.

Reflection _____

_____

Colleague

Ask a co-worker with whom you always meet at school to come to your home or to meet somewhere outside the school setting.

Reflection _____

_____

Group

Have each member on your team tell the group "One thing I did this summer for the first time."

Reflection _____

_____

Strategy 10 *Discover the importance of silence.*

Individual

On your way to work, if you always have the radio on, turn it off. Consider other places where you can control the noise level.

Reflection _____

_____

Colleague

In conversation with a co-worker, observe whether or not there are silent periods. When you ask a question of your co-worker, be quiet until you are sure they have finished their answer.

Reflection _____

_____

Group

In a brainstorming session, have everyone stop for five minutes and write their ideas. After five minutes, resume the discussion.

Reflection _____

_____

Fourth Key

ASKING QUESTIONS

It's better to know some of the questions than all of the answers.

James Thurber

ASKING QUESTIONS

What We Know

To ask questions is to inquire, to want more information, and to seek knowledge.

★ Asking questions demonstrates an interest in learning.

★ Posing questions with others can convey that we are open-minded.

★ To ask questions indicates a desire to move beyond the status-quo.

★ Pursuing answers to questions assists the development of our creativity.

★ Others feel empowered when we show interest by asking questions.

★ To inquire is to open the door to new possibilities.

Asking Questions – What We DO

WHAT WE OFTEN DO with KIDS	WHAT WE SOMETIMES DO with ADULTS
Wait until we have their attention	Ask when *we're* ready
Ask open ended questions	Ask closed ended questions
Ask questions with the intent of gaining new information	Ask questions to be "polite"
Find several ways to ask the same question	Use limited variations of questioning
Ask a lot of questions	Make more statements than inquiries
Welcome most of their questions	Become defensive in response to some of their questions
Ask varying levels of questions (e.g. knowledge, understanding, analysis, synthesis, evaluation, opinion)	Ask questions mostly at the knowledge level
Join them in asking questions	Ask questions "at them"
Ask questions that prompt reflective thinking	Ask questions that require little reflection

Strategies for Asking Questions

1. Increase your awareness of questioning behaviors.

2. In conversations/discussions balance question-asking with statement making.

3. Learn to ask open-ended questions.

4. Develop specific questions related to what the speaker is addressing.

5. Find ways to inquire that are perceived as non-threatening.

6. Take opportunities to find the meaning of a message by asking questions.

7. Become aware of the intent of questioning.

8. Recognize the value of questioning.

9. Use questioning as a method of gaining support from your colleagues.

10. Share your philosophical questions with colleagues.

Strategies and Practices for Asking Questions

Strategy 1 *Increase your awareness of questioning behaviors*

Individual

Pick one day at work to listen for questioning behaviors among the adults with whom you work. In the lounge, hallway and classrooms, what kinds of questions are being asked?

Reflection _____

_____

Colleague

When you meet in a planning session with a colleague, do you ask many questions? What kinds of questions? When given an answer, do you typically accept it at face value or ask another question?

Reflection _____

_____

Group

At a faculty or team meeting where a new rule or policy is being discussed, have everyone write down one question they have about the policy. Read a few of them aloud to the entire group. Discuss thoughts and opinions.

Reflection _____

_____

| Strategy 2 | **In conversations/discussions, balance question-asking with statement making.** |

Individual

After meeting with a co-worker, note how many questions you asked compared to how many statements you made. What's the difference between the two?

Reflection _____

_____

Colleague

Before meeting with a co-worker, decide that you will ask two questions to gain more understanding of what they are saying or thinking.

Reflection _____

_____

Group

Before an IEP meeting or child study meeting, ask each team member to write one question they have about the student. Post these questions so they are visible during the meeting.

Reflection _____

_____

Strategy 3   *Learn to ask open ended questions*

Individual

Pay attention to the questions you ask others. Can most questions be answered with just one word or with "yes" or "no"? How could you change your questions so the responses would be more informative?

Reflection _____

_____

Colleague

In preparation for a parent conference, write down all of the questions you have about how the student feels about school. Review the list and cross off all questions that could be answered by "yes" or "no." Ask one or two of the remaining questions at the conference.

Reflection _____

_____

Group

Begin an IEP or child-study meeting by asking the parent "Would you please tell us about your daughter? What likes, dislikes she has? How does she feel about school?"

Reflection _____

_____

| Strategy 4 | ***Develop specific questions related to what the speaker is addressing.*** |

Individual

As you listen to the principal speaking at a faculty meeting, write the questions that you have related to the topic. Note whether these questions are addressed.

Reflection _____

_____

Colleague

After a planning session with a co-worker, think about the questions that would have increased your understanding of your co-worker's ideas and suggestions. Try asking that type of question next time.

Reflection _____

_____

Group

At a committee or grade level meeting, when you are tempted to state your feelings about what is being said, instead ask a question about what is being said.

Reflection _____

_____

| Strategy 5 | *Find ways to inquire that are perceived as non-threatening* |

Individual

Write down all the ways you could ask someone how they feel about an idea of yours. Which sound the least threatening to you?

Reflection _____

_____

Colleague

Rather than ask a co-worker why they do something, ask for them to tell you how they do something and what led them to that practice.

Reflection _____

_____

Group

Have faculty or committee members discuss ways to ask questions of parents that would not be perceived as threatening.

Reflection _____

_____

Strategy 6 **Take opportunities to find the meaning of a message by asking questions.**

Individual

Listen to a talk show host for 15 minutes. Think of questions you could ask him or her to further clarify what was said.

Reflection _____

_____

Colleague

When a colleague tells you about something they're doing with students, ask how or if it is different from what they did when they first started teaching. How have they changed?

Reflection _____

_____

Group

When you have a guest speaker in your class, listen closely for statements the students may not understand. Raise your hand and ask questions that will cause the speaker to explain more fully.

Reflection _____

_____

Strategy 7   *Become aware of the intent of questioning*

Individual

As you hear yourself ask questions to others, determine the purpose of the question. Are the questions for the purpose of gaining information, getting permission, criticizing, or making a request?

Reflection _____

_____

Colleague

Write down questions other people ask you. What did they need from your answer? Was it clarification, validation, explanation, or information?

Reflection _____

_____

Group

Team members often ask parents "Do you have any questions?" What is the intent of this question? What might be a better question?

Reflection _____

_____

Strategy 8 *Recognize the value of questioning.*

Individual

Once a month, write down all of the questions you have about yourself as a professional. Keep these in a journal and refer to them from time to time.

Reflection _____

_____

Colleague

Ask a colleague, "If you could create your own school, what would it be like?"

Reflection _____

_____

Group

At the end of a faculty or team meeting, ask each person to express one question they still have about the issue discussed. Try not to answer these questions, just let them be heard by all.

Reflection _____

_____

| Strategy 9 | *Use questioning as a method of gaining support from your colleagues.* |

Individual

Think of something new you would like to try with your students. Ask a colleague to listen to the idea and provide feedback as to what the student response may be.

Reflection _____

_____

Colleague

After a planning session with a colleague, seek out two other people on the faculty to see if they know of human or material resources that would enhance your lesson.

Reflection _____

_____

Group

When procedural changes are going to occur, have the faculty answer the question: "How shall we communicate this to parents."

Reflection _____

_____

Strategy 10 *Share your philosophical questions with colleagues.*

Individual

Ask yourself, "Why did I originally choose to enter this profession?" and "Why am I choosing to continue in this profession and what do I want my legacy to be?"

Reflection _____

_____

Colleague

Ask a colleague, "What is the most rewarding part of this job for you?" and "What is the most difficult?" Then share your answers with them.

Reflection _____

_____

Group

Have team members read an article about student self-esteem. Discuss the article in relationship to what each of you believes about self-esteem.

Reflection _____

_____

Fifth Key

LISTENING

Nature has given us one tongue, but two ears, that we may hear from others twice as much as we speak.

Epictetus

LISTENING

What We Know

To listen is to make a conscious effort to hear
and to understand what is being said.

★   When we listen well and actively, the communication is more efficient and effective.

★   Listening can increase our understanding of diverse perspectives.

★   When we are good listeners, others feel more accepted in our presence.

★   The better we listen, the more we have opportunities for meaningful connections with others.

★   Listening is imperative to learning (we cannot learn if we do not listen).

LISTENING--What We DO

WHAT WE OFTEN DO with KIDS	WHAT WE SOMETIMES DO with ADULTS
Get down on their level (physically)	Remain on whatever level we begin the interaction
Give appropriate eye contact	Attempt to look at them and something else simultaneously
Attend well enough to ask questions related to what they just said	Attend enough so that we can make our next point
Allow the time they need to speak	Want their speaking pace to meet our needs
Listen for the feeling (emotions) behind the message	Take the words at "face value"
Watch for nonverbal cues along with what is said	Pay little attention to nonverbal cues
Give them our full attention	Attend to many things at once
Listen for messages/signs of understanding, growth, and change	Expect the messages to be of a "status quo" nature

Strategies for Listening

1. Learn to bring as much energy to listening as you do to speaking.

2. Establish routine checks to monitor listening behaviors.

3. Let others know when you need them as listeners.

4. Build listening times into established routines.

5. Learn to observe listening behaviors and their effects.

6. Increase awareness of selective listening.

7. Identify the barriers to effective listening.

8. Make conscious attempts to remove the barriers to effective listening.

9. Learn to attend to nonverbal messages.

10. Listen for the intent or purpose of a message.

Strategies and Practices for Listening

| Strategy 1 | *Learn to bring as much energy to listening as you do to speaking.* |

Individual

Identify settings where you tend to talk more than listen. Set a goal to increase your listening behavior in that setting.

Reflection _____

_____

Colleague

In your next interaction with a co-worker, make a conscious effort to listen well enough so that you can ask a question to further understand what was said.

Reflection _____

_____

Group

At a faculty meeting listen for and keep track of the number of questions asked as compared to statements made.

Reflection _____

_____

Strategy 2 *Establish routine checks to monitor listening behaviors.*

Individual

During an evening at home, check every 30 minutes to note what was the last thing you heard. Are you listening more to internal noise (self-talk) or external messages?

Reflection _____

_____

Colleague

In conversation with a colleague, begin to note when you start to "tune out" their message. What causes you to tune out?

Reflection _____

_____

Group

During a faculty meeting, check your watch every 10 minutes and note whether or not you can repeat what was last said and who said it.

Reflection _____

_____

Strategy 3   *Let others know when you need them as listeners.*

Individual

Think of a time when you just wanted someone to listen and instead they gave you advice. What could you say to them next time to prevent the advice giving?

Reflection _____

_____

Colleague

Think of ways to let another person know that you would appreciate their full attention as you tell them about an issue or concern.

Reflection _____

_____

Group

Before an interdisciplinary team meeting where parents will be present, ask your colleagues to listen for and record any jargon you use.

Reflection _____

_____

Strategy 4 *Build listening experiences into established routines.*

Individual

Take a minute several times a day to stop what you're doing and just listen to the sounds in your classroom.

Reflection _____

_____

Colleague

Make an audio recording of a student-parent conference with a parent (with permission, of course). When you play it back, listen for voice tone, interruptions, and the rate of speaking.

Reflection _____

_____

Group

Arrange for the faculty to hear a guest speaker from the community at one of the regular meetings.

Reflection _____

_____

Strategy 5 *Learn to observe listening behaviors and their effects*

Individual

Notice the behaviors you like in a listener. How close do you want them to be? Do you like it when they nod in understanding? What behaviors make you feel you aren't being listened to?

Reflection _____

_____

Colleague

In an important discussion with a co-worker, how do you demonstrate that you are listening? What do you do that seems to result in the person telling you more?

Reflection _____

_____

Group

When you are speaking to a large group, what behaviors indicate to you that people are listening? What behaviors lead you to believe people are not listening? How does that affect your message?

Reflection _____

_____

Strategy 6   *Increase awareness of selective listening.*

Individual

What radio stations do you listen to regularly? Why? What kinds of radio programs do you turn off? Why?

Reflection _____

_____

Colleague

When you talk with a co-worker, are there certain topics you listen to and remember? Are there other topics that you tune out almost immediately? Why?

Reflection _____

_____

Group

When discussing student progress, do you tend to listen better when others' results agree with yours? What happens to your listening skills when you hear results that conflict with yours?

Reflection _____

_____

Strategy 7 *Identify the barriers to effective listening*

Individual

Choose one day a week, for three weeks, and record events, people, or other distractions which interfere with your listening. Are they external factors or your own internal self-talk?

Reflection _____

_____

Colleague

What conditions in the school environment are interfering with effective listening during planning or team meetings with colleagues? Write down the ones that you can do something about.

Reflection _____

_____

Group

As a team, ask "What is the one thing we could do to improve our listening to parents?" After these are shared, ask "What is keeping us from doing these things?"

Reflection _____

_____

Strategy 8   *Make conscious attempts to remove the barriers to effective listening.*

Note: These practices are directly related to the previous Strategy 7-Practices 1-3

Individual

Of the barriers identified in *Strategy 7, Individual Practice Activity,* which barriers are within your control to remove or reduce? If they are external barriers, take steps to make changes in the setting. If they are internal barriers, replace the interfering self-talk with messages like "Remember to listen. Are you listening? What did he just say?"

Reflection _____

_____

Colleague

Make a commitment to remove barriers identified in *Strategy 7, Colleague Practice Activity.* Let your colleagues know that you are doing this so that you can give them your full attention, (e.g., let me close the door so I can pay attention to what you're saying).

Reflection _____

_____

Group

As a team, set a goal related to improving listening to parents. Review your progress regularly.

Reflection _____

_____

Strategy 9   *Learn to attend to nonverbal messages*

Individual

Turn on a favorite TV program. During the first five minutes watch the program with the volume turned down. Assess what you think is happening. Turn up the volume. Were you right?

Reflection _____

_____

Colleague

In a planning session with a colleague, notice the differences in voice tone and gestures. Do they become more animated as they discuss certain aspects? How do they non-verbally demonstrate their interest in what's being discussed?

Reflection _____

_____

Group

During a team meeting, if you see someone looking as though they are confused or puzzled, follow-up with a question like, "Mary, do you have a question or a comment?"

Reflection _____

_____

> ## Strategy 10 *Listen for the intent or purpose of a message.*

Individual

During a typical day, note the types of verbal interactions you have with your colleagues. Were the messages spoken for the purpose of polite social exchange, obtaining information, defending yourself or your opinion, explaining something, or just reporting?

Reflection _____

_____

Colleague

When people at work ask, "How are you?", do they have different reasons for asking the same question? Which ones are just asking to exchange greetings and which ones actually want you to tell them?

Reflection _____

_____

Group

Think of all the messages sent during an IEP meeting. Write down the different types (assessment reports, progress data, developmental history, health status). Discuss with the team the perceived purpose of the messages in these reports. Do they help or hinder communication?

Reflection _____

_____

Sixth Key

SPEAKING CLEARLY

It's not what you say, but how you say it that counts.

Robert Bolton
People Skills, 1979, Simon & Schuster.

SPEAKING CLEARLY

What We Know

To speak clearly is to send a message that is received
as it was meant.

★   When we learn to speak clearly we recognize that it is our responsibility to assure that effective communication has occurred.

★   Speaking clearly conveys a respect for the receiver and creates an atmosphere for mutual interaction.

★   When we learn to speak clearly, we learn to send messages that are more neutral in nature than judgmental.

★   The more clearly we learn to speak, the more likely the receiver will understand our message as we intended.

★   Learning to speak clearly will enhance the efficiency and effectiveness of our communication/collaboration interactions.

Speaking Clearly--What We DO

WHAT WE OFTEN DO with KIDS	WHAT WE SOMETIMES DO with ADULTS
Explain what we mean	Expect they'll understand what we mean
Use "I" messages	Use "you" or "they" messages
Tell them what we want or need	Keep our wants and needs to ourselves
Individualize our message based on student needs	Fail to consider the others' needs when we're speaking
Find many ways to explain ideas	Explain ideas in limited ways
Look for new vocabulary to enhance expression and understanding	Use the "same old words" in communication
Vary our pace according to the situation	Proceed at a similar pace most of the time, often in a hurry
Compliment them on their achievements	Fail to give them verbal recognition on their achievements.
Tell them when their behavior is having a negative effect	Tell someone else about their behavior when it is having a negative effect

Strategies for Speaking Clearly

1. Learn to use "I" messages.

2. Take responsibility for your spoken messages to be understood as you meant them.

3. Learn to request feedback regarding your spoken messages.

4. Become aware of the tone of your spoken messages.

5. Make it a habit to check for understanding during collaborative interactions.

6. Expand your speaking vocabulary.

7. Assess the situations where you have something to say yet avoid speaking.

8. Find ways to bring your voice to situations where you have avoided doing so.

9. Become a frequent observer of your speaking behaviors.

10. Identify and observe role models whose speaking you would like to emulate.

Strategies and Practices for Speaking Clearly

| Strategy 1 | *Learn to use "I" messages* |

Individual

Keep a journal for a month. Note all the controversial issues, questions, and dilemmas that arise. Practice writing "I" messages regarding the issues, i.e. "I believe….I would like…I think that…"

Reflection _____

_____

Colleague

When a co-worker speaks negatively to you about someone else and it makes you uncomfortable, say something like "Hmm, I really haven't experienced her in that way."

Reflection _____

_____

Group

Think about an aspect of your team or committee work that you do not believe is very effective. Bring it up at your next meeting by prefacing it with something like "I need to talk with you about _____ and get your ideas on how to improve our meetings."

Reflection _____

_____

Strategy 2 **_Take responsibility for your spoken messages to be understood as you meant them._**

Individual

Think about the way you express yourself when you are in a stressful situation. What are all the possible ways you might be misinterpreted? How could you begin to be clearer in those situations?

Reflection _____

_____

Colleague

In a discussion with a co-worker, after you've spoken at length about an issue, pause and ask something like, "It's important to me that I know if I'm making my ideas clear. Could you please tell me how I come across and what your understanding is of what I've been saying?"

Reflection _____

_____

Group

After an IEP meeting, arrange to meet with the parent(s) for 20 minutes or so. Explain to them that the team is working on improving communication skills and you would like their help. Discuss their understanding of what was said during the meeting and suggestions they might have to make it better.

Reflection _____

_____

Strategy 3   *Learn to request feedback regarding your spoken messages*

Individual

Write down several ways to request feedback such as "How did you think I came across? Did you hear me use any jargon in my report? Did I smile at the meeting?"

Reflection _____

_____

Colleague

Identify someone you talk with frequently and with whom you feel comfortable. Tell them you are working a specific area such as speaking more slowly. Ask them to notice you throughout the week and provide you with feedback from their observations.

Reflection _____

_____

Group

When you speak to a large group, ask the group to fill out a brief, anonymous questionnaire about your presentation. For example, have them rank you in the following areas: Getting to the Point, Making Eye Contact, and Speaking Loudly Enough.

Reflection _____

_____

> **Strategy 4**   *Become aware of the tone of your spoken messages.*

Individual

Turn on a cassette recorder in your room for a day. When you play it back, listen for your voice tone, pitch, pace, and volume. What patterns do you notice?

Reflection _____

_____

Colleague

During a conversation with a co-worker, try varying your speaking tone. For example, slow down when you want to make a point, speak softly as you convey concern, more loudly when you feel strongly about something. Note how each variation feels and whether or not it helps to convey the meaning.

Reflection _____

_____

Group

Notice your speaking tone at your departmental meetings. Do you speak up, emphasize what is important, ask questions, or leave the talking to everyone else?

Reflection _____

_____

Strategy 5	**Make it a habit to check for understanding during communication interactions.**

Individual

Write down all the ways you might ask, "Are you understanding what I'm saying?" Which ones feel the most natural for you to ask?

Reflection _____

_____

Colleague

Tell a colleague that you're working on speaking clearly so people understand you. Ask your colleague to let you know if you are talking too fast, or using expressions which may be confusing to others.

Reflection _____

_____

Group

During a team meeting where you are presenting an idea, ask the members to express their understanding of what you presented.

Reflection _____

_____

Strategy 6   *Expand your speaking vocabulary.*

Individual

Think of all the ways you can positively recognize someone else's efforts. Write them down; add to the list regularly.

Reflection _____

_____

Colleague

When you thank a colleague for something they have done, tell them specifically the effect their gesture had on you. For example, "Thanks for the note you left in my box. It made a hectic day a lot brighter."

Reflection _____

_____

Group

Brainstorm with a child study team the many different ways to describe a student's strengths. Keep the list posted and available for additions and use.

Reflection _____

_____

Strategy 7	**Assess the situations where you have something to say, yet avoid speaking.**

Individual

For one week at school, note the times you've wanted to speak up during the school day but did not. Where were these incidents happening; with whom; what was the topic?

Reflection _____

_____

Colleague

In relationship to your colleagues, are there some with whom you rarely share your opinions? What keeps you from sharing them?

Reflection _____

_____

Group

What is your comfort level speaking in large groups? Do you speak up in faculty meetings? What types of large groups are you least or most likely to speak? Why is this? Do you have any desire to change?

Reflection _____

_____

Strategy 8 **Find ways to bring your voice to situations where you have avoided doing so.**

Note: *These practices are directly related to Strategy 7, Practices 1-3*

Individual

From your observations in *Strategy 7, Individual Practice Activity*, choose one type of incident or one setting where you are going to speak up. Do it! Review later, "How did it feel? What was the effect?"

Reflection _____

_____

Colleague

Think of one colleague with whom you rarely share your opinions. Identify a topic that is important to you, but probably won't be controversial (e.g., recognizing student success). Tell your colleague that you've been trying to increase and expand the ways you recognize student success. Share some of your ideas and ask for theirs.

Reflection _____

_____

Group

Choose one type of large group that you'd like to speak up in but are hesitant to do so. Plan to say something at the next opportunity. Write down what you'll say. Practice in front of a mirror at home. Do it!

Reflection _____

_____

Strategy 9   *Become a frequent observer of your speaking behaviors*

Individual

What speaking habits do you have that interfere with com-medication? Do you say certain words or phrases so frequently that they've become meaningless? (e.g. "uh", "you know what I mean", or "ya know.")

Reflection _____

_____

Colleague

In a conversation with a co-worker who usually starts the discussion? Who talks the most? When you speak do you get right to the point or tend to beat around the bush? Do you talk too much, not enough, or just enough?

Reflection _____

_____

Group

When you become a part of a group, what is the pattern of your speaking behavior? Do you speak up right away or wait before saying anything. Do you speak comfortably with a lot of people you do not know? Is it easy for you to move from person to person and find things to talk about?

Reflection _____

_____

Strategy 10 *Identify and observe role models whose speaking you would like to emulate.*

Individual

Think of a personality (television, radio, theater) that you admire. What kind of voice do they have? Take an opportunity to listen and observe their voice tone, gestures, facial expressions, clarity, and speed with which they speak.

Reflection _____

_____

Colleague

Identify a co-worker who you believe has effective communication skills. For a week watch and listen for what it is that characterizes their speaking. Which of those characteristics could you improve? How?

Reflection _____

_____

Group

What teachers (or public speakers) do you know that are clearly outstanding in their ability to express themselves in large group situations. Identify the speaking traits that connect them with the audiences.

Reflection _____

_____

100 Ideas to
Reduce Stress and Increase Productivity
in Your Daily Teaching Life

Patty Lee, Ed.D.

Ten Tips for Each Topic:

Coping with Resistant Colleagues
Investing Rather than Expending Energy
Collaborating Effectively with Paraprofessionals
Disagreeing Tactfully
Using Nonjudgmental Language
Expressing Yourself
Asserting Yourself
Drawing Out the Best in Others
Not Taking Things Personally
and
Ten Suggestions for Tip Card Use

Ten Tips
for
Coping with Resistant Colleagues

* **Find the points on which you agree; articulate those points.**

* **Remember it is often the message that is resisted, not necessarily the messenger.**

* **Volunteer to serve on a committee together.**

* **Sit next to the person, not opposite, or across from them.**

* **Review students' records with your colleague.**

* **Find opportunities for your colleague to "tell you more" about something.**

* **Show authentic interest in an aspect of their teaching.**

* **Tell your colleague why you chose education as a profession.**

* **Recognize that you cannot change your colleague, but you can change *your* response.**

* **Remember you are an advocate for kids and resistance is normal.**

Ten Tips
for
Investing Rather than Spending your Energy

✳ **Participate regularly in activities that renew you.**

✳ **Recognize what you <u>can</u> do and put your energy there.**

✳ **Realize your job is infinite - FOCUS is important.**

✳ **Say "thank you" when someone compliments you.**

✳ **Identify activities you put off and yet are so glad once you do them. Do these more often.**

✳ **Learn a new skill.**

✳ **Hang out with positive energy people.**

✳ **Learn to tell your own stories to children.**

✳ **Give a sincere and specific compliment to a colleague.**

✳ **Do not say "yes" when you mean "no".**

Ten Tips
for
Collaborating Effectively with Paraprofessionals

✳ **Start and end each day with the paraprofessional.**

✳ **Provide the paraprofessional with constructive feedback ASAP.**

✳ **Say "thank you" frequently for specific acts.**

✳ **Ask the paraprofessional how *you* can help.**

✳ **Demonstrate what you mean.**

✳ **Recognize the individual and unique contributions of each paraprofessional.**

✳ **Occasionally meet together away from the school or work area.**

✳ **Encourage the paraprofessional to keep a daily journal of activities, thoughts, and feelings.**

✳ **Ask the paraprofessional what they would like to learn.**

✳ **Advocate for the paraprofessional's professional growth.**

Ten Tips
for
Disagreeing Tactfully

* Find the points on which you agree and state them.

* Use the word "and" more frequently than "but".

* Post points of discussion on a flip chart. Note the areas of disagreement.

* Have each person write their opinion; read the opinions aloud.

* Find your own way of saying, "I disagree". For example, "I see it differently."

* State your opinion about the topic, *not* the other person.

* Restate what you understand others to be saying.

* Think before you speak.

* Find support for your viewpoint.

* Recognize when you are willing to compromise and when you are not.

Ten Tips
for
Using Nonjudgmental Language

✳ Avoid using the words _always_ and _never_.

✳ Use "_yes, and_" rather than "_yes, but_".

✳ Ask people to tell you more; elaborate.

✳ Put as much energy into listening as you do speaking.

✳ Expect and welcome different points of view.

✳ Ask "_how_" and not "_why_".

✳ Give the ideas some "_think time_".

✳ Explain differences (rather than compare).

✳ Recognize your own "_need to be right_".

✳ Remember "_right_" is relative.

Ten Tips
for
Expressing Yourself

* **Write down what you want to say.**

* **Practice expressing yourself to a friend.**

* **Visualize yourself speaking with confidence.**

* **Take a deep breath before you speak.**

* **Remember you may be speaking for others who share the same opinion.**

* **Record your personal speaking experiences in a journal.**

* **Observe others who speak up and note the qualities you admire.**

* **Tape record yourself stating your opinion about an issue.**

* **Listen to the tape recording and note where your voice is strongest.**

* **Write ten ways to express the same message.**

Ten Tips
for
Asserting Yourself

✳ **Use "I" statements.**

✳ **Don't preface your statement with an apology.**

✳ **Identify your role models of assertiveness. Note the qualities you would like to develop.**

✳ **Recognize where your opinion is different; state it.**

✳ **Check out your understanding of others' messages.**

✳ **Don't put down another person's opinion; simply state your own.**

✳ **Remember you are disagreeing about an issue, not competing with the other person.**

✳ **Give yourself a time-out from the discussion. Regroup.**

✳ **Give a sincere and specific compliment to a colleague.**

✳ **Do not say "yes" when you really mean "no".**

Ten Tips
for
Drawing Out the Best in Others

✳ **Ask others for their ideas and opinions.**

✳ **Listen well enough to ask related questions about the topic.**

✳ **Request their help when brainstorming about a current issue.**

✳ **Check to see that you understand where they are "coming from".**

✳ **Share common interests.**

✳ **When you have questions or need to discuss an issue, ask when the best time is to meet.**

✳ **Compliment others in authentic and specific ways.**

✳ **Observe what times of day are best for individual interactions.**

✳ **Put as much energy into listening to others, as you do when speaking to others.**

✳ **Encourage others to expand or elaborate on topics which they initiate.**

Ten Tips
for
Not Taking Things Personally

* Many statements are disguised as questions. You don't have to answer them.

* Ask for the meaning of the message to be clarified.

* The message usually says more about the speaker than about you.

* You are not responsible for the whole world.

* The speaker would probably say this to a number of people-you just happen to be the immediate receiver.

* Visualize a cartoon caricature of the person; don't take it so seriously.

* Reassure yourself like you would reassure a friend.

* Ask the person if they meant it the way you took it.

* Increase your response-_ability_ not your responsibility.

* People are more often upset with the situation than with _you_.

Tips for Effective Collaboration
Suggestions for Use

* Photocopy the Tip Cards on colored paper, laminate and post.

* Select a Tip Card as a "Feature of the Month". Try one or two suggestions. Note the results.

* Use one of the Tip Cards as a topic for discussion at a faculty meeting.

* As a recognition tool, give Tip Cards to people who demonstrate these abilities.

* Design professional development goals related to the tips.

* Ask team, committee, or task force members to choose areas which they would like to improve.

* Practice tip suggestions with students first, then colleagues.

* Reflect on why some tips are easy for you and others more difficult.

* Write your own tips for something you want to improve.

* Maintain a journal reflecting your progress toward your individual goals.

Use this page to write down ideas that might come to mind while reading/referring to this guide.
Remember, collaboration begins with each one of us making ourselves accessible to others.

AFTERWORD

This book is written to stress the importance of conducting ourselves in a respectful and interdependent manner as we face the future. We must realize that we are all in this together for the good of the students. I hope this book has shed light upon the many strategies and practices that contribute to more collaboration among educators, parents, students, and the community. Perhaps it has prompted additional ideas, which you are able to carry out in your particular setting. As educators we are positive role models for the students in our care and the way we communicate with other adults' sets an example of effective communication and productive problem solving for our students. Students are impressed by how they see us behave and in what they hear us say.

Effective Communication depends upon our implementation of the following of six keys: *Developing Expectations, Preparing Ahead, Understanding Perspectives, Asking Questions, Listening,* and *Speaking Clearly.* When we are able to do all of these effectively, we contribute to an overall purpose of providing a healthy learning environment for our students.

A Note from the Author

It has been an absolute delight to write this book! I have taught classes, seminars, and workshops in collaboration and communication for 25 years, and my students continue to be my greatest resource. I am available to conduct workshops and staff development opportunities for school districts nationally and internationally. With over 40 years of experience as a Speech Therapist, Counselor, Educator, Special Education Director, and as an Associate Professor, I would be happy to assist you with the development of collaborative practices in your unique setting.

Also, if you have additional ideas you would like considered for a future publication, please write to me at either of the addresses listed below. Best wishes and good luck!

Patty Lee, Ed.D.
10 Quedo Rd.
Santa Fe, NM 87508
pleesf@comcast.net

GLOSSARY

Child Study Team - A group of general and special educators who meet on a regular basis to review and discuss students who are experiencing difficulty in school. In some settings this team serves as a pre-referral special education team. It may also be referred to as an Intervention Team, Referral Team, or Teachers Assisting Teachers (TAT) Team.

Colleague - Any adult working in the school setting in the interest of students. For the purpose of this publication, the words *Colleague* and *Co-Worker* are used interchangeably.

Committee Meeting - A meeting comprised of staff members working together to address a specific issue. Some school districts use additional terminology such as Focus Team, Curriculum Team, Site-Based Management Team, and so forth.

IEP - The Individualized Education Program is a legal document developed for a student who qualifies for Special Education Services. Different states require different membership on this team. The team usually includes: General Educator, Administrator, Special Educator, Parent, Student, and any additional school personnel who have been involved in the assessment of the student.

Interdisciplinary Team - A team that is responsible for carrying out the identification of students who are eligible for Special Services. It often includes but is not limited to the General Educator, Special Educator, School

Psychologist, Nurse, Counselor, Various Specialists (Speech/Language, Occupational Therapist, and Social Worker).

Staffing - A meeting held to develop an Individualized Educational Program (IEP). The members are invited to attend the meeting. This meeting may also be referred to as an Assessment Summary Meeting, Initial IEP Meeting, IEP Information Session, or IEP Placement Meeting.

Notes.

Notes.

Notes.

Notes.

Notes.

Notes.

Notes.

CORWIN PRESS

The Corwin Press logo—a raven striding across an open book—represents the union of courage and learning. Corwin Press is committed to improving education for all learners by publishing books and other professional development resources for those serving the field of PreK–12 education. By providing practical, hands-on materials, Corwin Press continues to carry out the promise of its motto: **"Helping Educators Do Their Work Better."**